# How To Open Your Next Negotiation

*How To Start A Negotiation In Order To Get The Best Possible Outcome*

*"Practical, proven techniques that will help you open a negotiation the right way in order to get a better deal"*

**Dr. Jim Anderson**

Published by:
Blue Elephant Consulting
Tampa, Florida

Copyright © 2013 by Dr. Jim Anderson

All rights reserved. No part of this book may be reproduced of transmitted in any form or by any means, electronic or mechanical, including photocopying, recording or by any information storage and retrieval system without written permission of the publisher, except for inclusion of brief quotations in a review.

Printed in the United States of America

Library of Congress Control Number: 2013921143

ISBN-13: 978-1493759798
ISBN-10:1493759795

**Warning – Disclaimer**

The purpose of this book is to educate and entertain. This book does not promise or guarantee that anyone following the ideas, tips, suggestions, techniques or strategies will be successful. The author, publisher and distributor(s) shall have neither liability nor responsibility to anyone with respect to any loss or damage caused, or alleged to be caused, directly or indirectly by the information contained in this book.

# Other Books By The Author

**Product Management**

- How To Have A Successful Product Manager Career: The Things That You Need To Be Doing TODAY In Order To Have A Successful Product Manager Career

- Product Manager Product Success: How to keep your product on track and make it become a success

**Public Speaking**

- Secrets To Planning The Perfect Speech

- Secrets To Organizing The Perfect Speech: How to organize the best speech of your life!

**CIO Skills**

- CIO Business Skills: How CIOs can work effectively with the rest of the company!

- Managing Your CIO Career: Steps That CIOs Have To Take In Order To Have A Long And Successful Career

### IT Manager Skills

- IT Manager Budgeting Skills

- IT Manager Career Secrets: Tips And Techniques That IT Managers Can Use In Order To Have A Successful Career

### Negotiating

- Preparing For Your Next Negotiation: What You Need To Do BEFORE A Negotiation Starts In Order To Get The Best Possible Deal

### Miscellaneous

- Power Distribution Unit (PDU) Secrets: What Everyone Who Works In A Data Center Needs To Know!

- Making The Jump: How To Land Your Dream Job When You Get Out Of College!

# **Acknowledgements**

Any book like this one is the result of years of real-world work experience. In my over 25 years of working for 7 different firms, I have met countless fantastic people and I've been mentored by some truly exceptional ones. Although I've probably forgotten some of the people who made me the person that I am today, here is my attempt to finally give them the recognition that they so truly deserve:

- Thomas P. Anderson
- Art Puett
- Bobbi Marshall
- Bob Boggs

Dr. Jim Anderson

*This book is dedicated to my wife Lori. None of this would have been possible without her love and support.*

*Thanks for the best 21 years of my life (so far)...!*

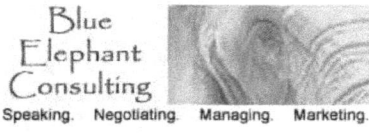

Speaking.  Negotiating.  Managing.  Marketing.

# Table Of Contents

IT'S ALL ABOUT THE OPENING .......................................................... 8

ABOUT THE AUTHOR ................................................................... 10

CHAPTER 1: DEAL + NEGOTIATION = CONTRACT (OR THE FOUR MODES TO GET YOU THERE!) ......................................................... 14

CHAPTER 2: THREE SECRETS THAT HAVE BEEN MISSING FROM NEGOTIATION TRAINING ............................................................... 17

CHAPTER 3: THE OTHER SIDE OF NEGOTIATION: PERSUASION ......... 21

CHAPTER 4: BODY LANGUAGE SKILLS THAT WOMEN DON'T KNOW ABOUT ............................................................................................ 24

CHAPTER 5: DOES YOUR BODY LANGUAGE MUMBLE? .................... 28

CHAPTER 6: THE DELICATE ART OF USING PERSUASION IN NEGOTIATIONS ............................................................................... 32

CHAPTER 7: BOTH WIN: HOW TO NEGOTIATE A BETTER DEAL FOR BOTH PARTIES ................................................................................ 35

CHAPTER 8: 3 NEGOTIATION TIPS FROM THE MASTER: DONALD TRUMP ............................................................................................ 38

CHAPTER 9: 10 TIPS FOR GETTING SATISFACTION WHILE NEGOTIATING ................................................................................. 41

CHAPTER 10: 7 WAYS TO BE SUCCESSFUL IN A NEGOTIATION ......... 44

CHAPTER 11: 3 STEPS TO BUILDING A BETTER NEGOTIATION .......... 48

CHAPTER 12: 8 INGREDIENTS FOR BAKING A DELICIOUS NEGOTIATION ................................................................................. 51

## It's All About The Opening

Every negotiation starts with an opening. It's what we all do at the start of a negotiation. What a lot of us don't realize is that how we handle the opening of a negotiation can have a big impact on how the rest of the negotiation goes. The very possibility of success may hinge on how we start things off.

There are a number of different factors that go into opening your next negotiation correctly. You need to be able to read the body language of the negotiating team that is sitting across from you: are they under pressure to reach a deal, or do they have all the time in the world?

Negotiation has a flip side and its name is persuasion. Understanding what persuasion is and, more importantly, how best to use it during a negotiation can go a long way in helping you to change the other side's view and what they are willing to agree to.

It can be very easy to focus completely on the negotiations that are happening right now. However, as negotiators we need to be able to see the "big picture". We will probably negotiate with the other side again at some point in the future.

What this means for us is that we have a responsibility for making sure that when the negotiation is over and done with, both sides leave the table with a feeling of satisfaction. Although important, just exactly how we make this happen can at times be challenging.

The end result of being ready for the opening of your next negotiation is that when you sit down at the negotiating table, you'll have a sense of being prepared. You'll have the ability to understand how you are going to connect with the other side of the table and you'll have a plan for ensuring that both parties walk away from the table with a sense of satisfaction. This is exactly what you're going to need in order to be able to reach the type of deal that will allow you to believe that you accomplished what you showed up to do.

For more information on what it takes to be a great negotiator, check out my blog, The Accidental Negotiator, at:

www.TheAccidentalNegotiator.com

Good luck!

- Dr. Jim Anderson, November, 2013

## About The Author

I must confess that I never set out to be a negotiator. When I went to school, I studied Computer Science and thought that I'd get a nice job programming and that would be that. Well, at least part of that plan worked out!

My first job was working for Boeing on their F/A-18 fighter jet program. I spent my days programming fighter jet software in assembly language and I loved it. The U.S. government decided to save some money and went looking for other countries to sell this plane to. This put me into an unfamiliar role: I started to negotiate with foreign military officials and I ended up having to participate in the negotiations for large international deals.

Time moved on and so did I. I found myself working for Siemens, the big German telecommunications company. They were making phone switches and selling them to the seven U.S. phone companies. The problem was that the switches were too complicated. When it came time to negotiate a deal with the customer, the sales teams struggled to create an effective negotiating strategy. I was called in to bridge the world between the product functionality and the business impacts as they related to the negotiations.

I've spent over 25 years working as a negotiator for both big companies and startups. This has given me an opportunity to learn what it takes to both plan and execute negotiations of all sizes. When it comes to negotiations, I've pretty much been there, done that.

I now live in Tampa Florida where I spend my time managing my consulting business, Blue Elephant Consulting, teaching college courses at the University of South Florida, and traveling to work with companies like yours to share the knowledge that I have about how to prepare for and execute successful negotiations.

I'm always available to answer questions and I can be reached at:

Dr. Jim Anderson
Blue Elephant Consulting
Email: jim@BlueElephantConsulting.com
Facebook: http://goo.gl/1TVoK
Web: http://www.BlueElephantConsulting.com/

**"Unforgettable communication skills that will set your ideas free..."**

# Create An Effective Negotiating Team At Your Company!

Dr. Jim Anderson is available to provide training and coaching on the topics that are the most important to people who have to negotiate: how can my team effectively prepare for and execute a successful negotiation that will get us what we both want and need?

Dr. Anderson believes that in order to both learn and remember what he says, audiences need to laugh. Each one of his speeches is full of fun and humor so that what he says "sticks" with everyone.

### Dr. Anderson's Negotiating Training Includes:

1. How to plan for a negotiation: what information do you need and where can you find it?

2. What's the best way to explore how a deal can be created during a negotiation?

3. How can you bring a negotiation to a close without giving in to the other side?

Dr. Jim Anderson works with over 100 customers per year. To invite Dr. Anderson to work with you, contact him at:

**Phone: 813-418-6970** or
**Email: jim@BlueElephantConsulting.com**

Speaking. Negotiating. Managing. Marketing.

# Chapter 1

## Deal + Negotiation = Contract (or the Four Modes To Get You There!)

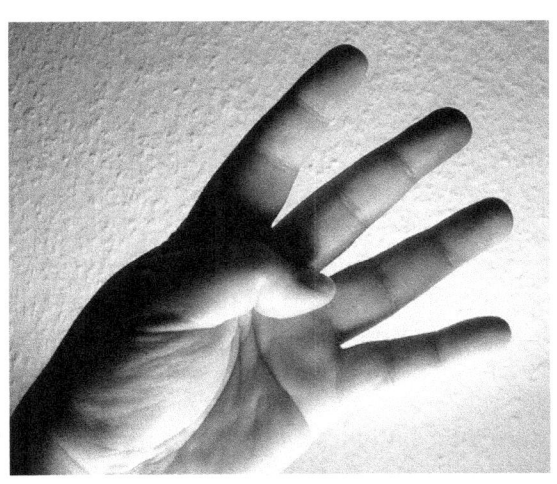

# Chapter 1: Deal + Negotiation = Contract (or the Four Modes To Get You There!)

Too many people look at a negotiation in a negative way. They sigh, and instantly become tired whenever the prospect of entering into a negotiation shows up. What they are missing is that a negotiation is not necessarily a contest. When there is a deal to be done or a contract to be signed, then negotiation skills are required.

The secret to getting the best deals from your next negotiation is to realize that just like the different roles that you have to play as a skilled negotiator, there are four modes of negotiating that arise during each negotiation session. If you can learn to recognize these modes and come up with ways to deal with them, then you'll know how to deal with them. Here are brief descriptions of the four modes, let's see how many you recognize:

- **The Cooperative Mode (Both Win):** During this phase, both parties realize that there is a better deal available to both of them if they are both willing to take the time and make the effort to look for it. They will know that they have found it when both sides have increased their profit and/or their satisfaction without harming the other side.

- **The Competitive Mode (Defending Your Interests)**: During this phase you are locked in a competitive battle with the other side. There will be a winner and a loser and you'll be darned if you are going to be the loser! During this phase, you should say as little as possible because information is power and you don't want to give too much power to the other side.

- **The Organizational Mode:** This is very much like the "channeling" that mystics do for folks who have passed on to the spirit world. The other side is really representing their organization and because of this their hands are tied on some matters.

    When they say "No" it may not be the other negotiator that is saying it, but rather his/her organization that is saying it. During your preparation for negotiation make sure that you know the other side's organizational structure and what pressures they will place on their negotiator.

- **The Personal Mode**: The ultimate goal of any negotiation is for both parties to walk away feeling satisfied. What it's going to take to satisfy the other side may lie buried beneath the actual issues that are being discussed. Your job as a negotiator is to be aware of your "satisfaction issues" and to uncover the other side's.

There you have it. You've probably seen all four of these modes in play during your past negotiations; however, you may not have seen yourself in these modes also. Knowing that they exist and molding your reactions to them will help to make you a more successful negotiator.

# Chapter 2

---

# Three Secrets That Have Been Missing From Negotiation Training

# Chapter 2: Three Secrets That Have Been Missing From Negotiation Training

This is going to be a bit of a rant, so I should probably apologize for that in advance.

Over the past 10 years I have read countless books on negotiating, attended training course after training course, and in the end I was left feeling that something very fundamental was missing — there were secrets to being a successful negotiator that weren't being talked about. There is nothing more frustrating than knowing that you don't know something. I knew that I needed to find somebody who knew these secrets and who would be willing to share them with me.

When in doubt, talk to Sales. So that's what I did – I started going out on customer visits with every salesperson that would let me tag along. What I saw was that there were good sales people and bad sales people.

The good sales people would dive into a negotiation with a customer, tussle about the details, and in the end they would emerge with an agreement that was good for their company and with a satisfied customer no matter what they had gotten or given up.

The bad sales people would enter a negotiation as though they were jumping into a street fight, have a knock-down-drag-out with the customer, and finally emerge bruised with a bad agreement and an angry customer. So what were they doing differently?

The bad sales people had clearly gone to the same negotiating classes that I had attended. They used the same negotiating vocabulary that I used and they stepped though a negotiation using the basic steps that I was currently using. They couldn't really teach me anything. It was the good sales people who held the negotiating secrets that I was looking for.

As I focused on what the good sales people were doing, it very slowly dawned on me that they were being successful because of things that they were doing that weren't taught in any negotiating course that I had ever taken. This clearly called for some serious beer conversations in order to gain access to these secrets.

Over way too many beers, I was eventually able to tease the answers out of the really good sales people about how they were so successful in negotiating with their customers. At a very high level, what they told me was that I had been missing the other side of the negotiation coin: **persuasion**.

What they said is that negotiating is basically convincing someone to do something. What the bad sales people are missing is the other half of the process: persuading the customer that this is what they want. In fact, if you are good at persuasion then the customer will be falling all over themselves to buy what you have.

As I took all of this in, it started to become clear that what the good sales people were doing could be broken into three main sets of skills:

- **Rapport**: they developed a sense of bonding with their customers that allowed the customers to treat them not like "the other side of the table", but rather like an old friend that they were meeting once again.

- **Body Language**: just like a cheerleader, the good sales people realized that in addition to the words that were coming out of their mouths, their bodies were also talking to the customer and they made sure that what their bodies were saying matched what their mouths were saying.

- **Knowing What To Say & When To Say It**: the bad sales people always seemed to have periods of awkward silence when they met with customers. The good sales people, on the other hand, always seemed to have something to say and it always seemed to get a positive response out of the customer.

There is a lot more to this persuasion stuff; however, for now understand that even if you think that you know everything about negotiating, if you don't have the persuasion skills that you need, then you still have a lot to learn!

# Chapter 3

# The Other Side Of Negotiation: Persuasion

# Chapter 3: The Other Side Of Negotiation: Persuasion

The last time that I went into an auto dealership to buy a car, I was smart enough to keep my eyes open. Because I realized that I was entering into a negotiating "combat zone", I wanted to see what the dealer would do to prepare me for the inevitable pricing discussions that we were going to be having.

Although I came ready to negotiate, what I discovered is that even before we began to talk, the dealer was trying to persuade me to buy a car there. Suddenly the light turned on for me – there's a whole dimensional to this negotiating stuff that I had not realized was there…

The ultimate goal of any negotiation is to convince the other side to do what you want them to do: sell you the car, buy your house, give you a job, sign the contract, etc. We've spent some time talking about what I like to call "classical negotiating". This includes preparing to negotiate, planning on what you are going to compromise on, and even how to deal with demands and deadlines. Now it's time to talk about the other side of the coin: **persuasion**.

Persuasion is one of those words that we all know, but would be hard pressed to define. To put it simply, persuasion is a form of social influence in which one party guides another party to a conclusion or action. This is accomplished by appealing to the other party's needs and wants instead of forcing them to do something. If taken too far, then persuasion can turn into manipulation where only one party benefits from the interaction.

Why take the time to talk about persuasion when we really should be talking about negotiation? Simple, the two forms of communication are different sides to the same coin. I like to think about persuasion as being the unspoken part of negotiation. In a perfect world, if you could persuade the other side to sell you the car, buy your house, sign the contract, then that would be all that was needed. However, often persuasion is not enough, and that's when negotiation comes in to play. No matter how things turn out, persuasion has a role to play before, during, and after a negotiation.

When communicating with the other side, there are two basic forms of persuasion that can be used: logical and emotional. It's important to realize that both forms are often used together – this is not an either or situation.

The logical appeal attempts to use facts, logic, and reason to convince the other party to agree to take some action. The emotional appeal attempts to capture the other side's imagination, their heart, or simply to appeal to their belief system to achieve the same thing.

Back to that car dealer. The walls of the dealership were covered with facts & stats about the safety and gas mileage of the cars that I was looking at (logical). They had pictures up around the place of past customers with little hand written notes that thanked the dealership for their service and support (emotional/social).

Finally, when I sat down with the salesman to talk about pricing, I couldn't help but notice the oversized picture of his wife and children that was prominently displayed on his desk (emotional). Next time you get ready to negotiate; don't forget to prepare for the other 50% of your task – persuasion!

# Chapter 4

# Body Language Skills That Women Don't Know About

# Chapter 4: Body Language Skills That Women Don't Know About

Negotiating is simply a form of specialized communication. We've mentioned that persuasion is the flip side of negotiation – the non-verbal communication skills that go along with negotiation's spoken words. Body language – what our bodies are telling the other side, is a key part of this persuasion skill.

What's interesting is that men seem to do a better job of using their persuasion skills than women do as a part of any deal making. Why is this? I'm sure that psychologists would have a lot to say about it; however, let's just assume the root cause is how we were all brought up.

Boys have been taught to do everything possible to win – no holds barred while girls are taught that there are boundaries that should not be mixed or crossed. Let's see what we can do about straightening this all out…

As we start the 21st century with its global workforce, new competitors, and changing workplace rules, I believe that persuasion skills are the one set of skills that will set the high achievers apart from everyone else. Some people are just born with a natural ability to communicate well with everyone they meet.

The rest of us have to work at it. Just to make things even more complicated, I'm here to tell you that it's still a "man's world". Men still run businesses and most of us are working for a man either directly or somewhere in our management chain.

As a man, this is great news for me because I know how to communicate with men. I've been around men all my life and they communicate exactly the same way I do. However, it's not always so easy for women to talk to men , both in the workplace and in your personal lives. Let's solve that problem.

I'm going to give you the skills that you need to understand what both men and women are really telling you and I'm going to show you how you can clearly communicate your message to them at the same time.

Now I've got a confession to make – earlier in my career I got canned, fired, walked to the door, call it what you will, you get the point. I'd like to say that I'm a master communicator and that I knew that this was coming; however, that's not the case.

This firing completely blind-sided me. I did not see it coming. Now I thought that I was very good at reading people; however, I was not looking in the right places and that's one of the reasons that I got taken by surprise.

Since then I have honed my people skills so that I never again get surprised: now I am much better at telling what someone is really thinking and I don't get confused by their words. This is the skill that I'm going to be passing on to you.

To get things started, let's talk about body language. We all know what this is, but how often do we remember to use it in every conversation that we have?

To get started, you need to change your thinking about every conversation that you have each day. Think about each conversation that you have as being like having three simultaneous phone calls going on with the person that you are talking to: your words, your tone, and your body language.

This understanding is important because not only do you need to understand what other people are saying to you, you also have to understand that you are sending multiple messages simultaneously when you speak to others. What is your body language saying about you?

We ignore these gestures because we are so self-involved in what we are saying and trying to listen to what the other person is saying. A quick word of caution: a single isolated gesture is like a single word , doesn't mean anything unless you put it in context in which it is being used.

Just because someone is tugging on their ear when they are talking to you, does not necessarily mean anything! When studying body language, a key point is that it's when there is change in someone's gestures that we should take notice. When they start to make a new gesture that indicates that they have just started to feel some way.

Where did I get all of this wonderful information? It's been picked up from watching and observing my coworkers over time & doing lots & lots of reading on the subject. We all need to realize that in any negotiation situation the non-verbal communication is as important as words being used.

# Chapter 5

---

# Does Your Body Language Mumble?

# Chapter 5: Does Your Body Language Mumble?

Ah body language, the secret communications channel that we couldn't turn off if we wanted to. When we are negotiating it's important to remember that your body is giving off all sorts of signals that you may or may not want it to be sending.

I'm not sure if you can prevent your personal body language from stuttering or mumbling like you can your spoken words, but the good news is that you are not the only one talking this way. The other side is also giving you many clues as to what they are thinking and what their next move might be.

If you are attuned to watch for and read the other side's body language, then you just might find yourself in the driver's seat for this negotiation. Let's see if we can decode some of the messages that are being sent your way:

- **Key point**: it's when there is change in someone's gestures that we should take notice. When they start to make a new gesture this is what indicates that they have just started to feel some way. Don't get hung up by individual gestures, rather focus on groups of gestures – they are the ones that are really telling you a story.

- **Our (and their) attitude is formed by initial interaction with people**: We quickly form an attitude of openness or attitude of defensiveness. Keep your eyes open and pick up on these initial body gestures when you first meet the other side.

Let's talk about some single gestures. Remember, don't fret about these if you see them individually, it's when you see them in groups that they are really sending you a message:

- **Cooperation & agreement**: Gestures that expose the body imply trust, communicate "yes", obvious and meant to be seen. Arms away from the body or over the head are a good example of this.

- **Slow & deliberate gestures**: Open hands show a willingness to meet the situation. Uncrossed arms and legs are another good example of this.

- **Moving forward**: in negotiations we really like to see these gestures because they indicate that we're going to make some progress – Hands on hips , feet apart. Often the signs of a high achiever, or a go-getter who wants to reach a negotiated agreement.

- **Hands on chest:**, this is a way to reinforce sincerity

- **Rubbing palms**: shows both eagerness & expectancy

- **Appraisal & interest**: there are a lot of ways to show this, one of the more common is when the head is tilted.

- **Hand to cheek gestures**: Chin in hand, finger along bottom - evaluating what we are saying with interest, calm evaluation. Stroking the chin - making a decision about what you are saying

- **Interest In The Conversation**: more interest  - leaning forward you , I'm with you. Less interest  - leaning back, away from you.

- **Confidence**: good eye contact, steepling with fingers , higher up from lap. More confidant (up by the eyes , too confidant!) - hand in packet w/ a finger out. Confidence - hands laced behind the head. Confidence - legs crossed also means they are feeling quite smug.

There you have it – a laundry list of body gestures that you can look for during your next negotiation. Remember that the other side is probably going to be focused on the actual steps in the negotiation and may not be working to pick up on your body language. If so, you've just found a great advantage that just might help you to come out ahead!

# Chapter 6

# The Delicate Art Of Using Persuasion In Negotiations

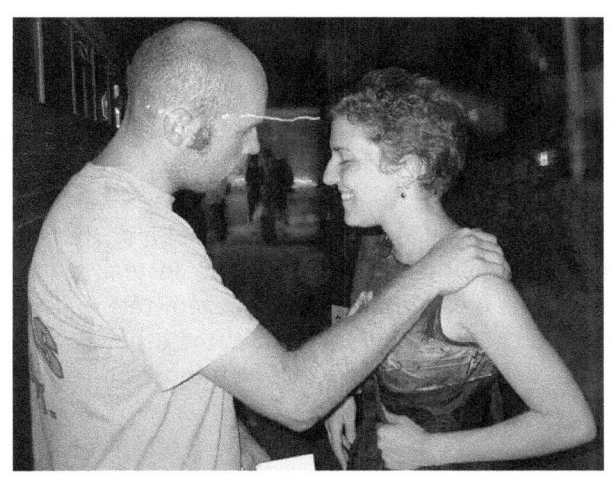

# Chapter 6: The Delicate Art Of Using Persuasion In Negotiations

So why do we even bother negotiating with the other side? The answer is simple: we need the other side to do or provide us with what we want. Study after study has shown that most people (this includes me) believe that we're so smart that nobody can sell anything to us.

Good negotiators know that the truth turns out to be that we can be persuaded to do something if, and only if, we don't recognize that the other side is using a "sales" technique on us. Why should this matter to you?

Simple – when you are negotiating with the other side and you take the time to use a few persuasion techniques then you will be taking advantage of what modern psychological research has revealed about how we can make our ideas and negotiating positions more credible and more believable. Let's talk about how you can accomplish this…

**Use a rifle, not a shotgun**: If you want the other side to accept your ideas and make them their own, you need to aim at a narrow target. This means that you need to stop doing what we all instinctively do during a negotiation: back the truck up and dump all of the information that we've collected about our position all over the other side.

It turns out that this will just end up overwhelming them and not do much to bring them over to our side. Instead, what you should do is some field work before you even start to negotiate. You need to find out what's important to the other side. This will allow you to focus your persuasion on those and only those points.

**Make It Story Time**: Stories are a fantastic way for us to learn and they can be very effective way to persuade someone. However, if it sounds like you are giving a sales pitch, then you can be assured that telling a story won't work.

Instead, if you focus on a story that has real meaning, then the other side's unconscious mind will automatically draw the necessary connections without any help from you and the result will be that they end up doing the persuasion for you. The key to telling an effective story is to once again pinpoint what matters to the other side and then tell a story about a similar idea or concept. This indirect approach is the secret to winning the other side over to your way of thinking and keeps them from feeling like you are using a hard sell technique on them.

# Chapter 7

## Both Win: How To Negotiate A Better Deal For Both Parties

# Chapter 7: Both Win: How To Negotiate A Better Deal For Both Parties

The phrase "win-win" is looking pretty ragged along about now. How about if we talk about the much more meaningful "both win" strategy for negotiating?

The key to creating a successful both-win negotiation is to remember that at its heart, negotiation is all about sharing value between both parties. If it was as simple as that, we really wouldn't need this book!

However, as human beings we often use one of two different approaches when we enter into a negotiation: competitive mode or cooperative mode. Can you guess which mode most of us enter a negotiation with?

When we are in the competitive mode, we focus on who is currently getting how much of the pie. When we are in the cooperative mode, we focus on trying to make the pie larger so that everyone will walk away with more. Clearly the cooperative mode is the route to creating a both-win deal for both parties.

So all of this discussion leads to the big issue: how can we go about creating a both-win deal when we always seem to start out in competitive mode? The answer is that we need to start asking ourselves the right types of questions.

Specifically, we need to ask the questions that will allow us to find out what things can be changed that will allow both sides of the table's interests better. A good example of how to do this is when you start to talk about schedules for what you are negotiating.

If you can either receive or deliver the thing that is being negotiated earlier, later, or maybe all at one time or even in parts then all of a sudden there is additional value to share with both parties.

One additional way to cause this shift in negotiating modes to occur is to find a way to communicate to the other side of the table that you really WANT to reach an agreement with them, not that you HAVE to. Doing this and helping them feel good about it will go a long way towards allowing you to reach your negotiating goals.

If you are able to shift the negotiation from the competitive mode to the cooperative mode, then you will have greatly improved your chances of reaching a negotiated agreement. It's not always easy to do, but I think that you'll find the results well worth the effort.

# Chapter 8

## Negotiation Tips From The Master: Donald Trump

# Chapter 8: 3 Negotiation Tips From The Master: Donald Trump

I believe that by now we all probably have somewhat of a love / hate relationship with Donald Trump ("The Donald" if you like). No matter how you feel about the guy, you have to give him credit – he's done quite well for himself.

What's interesting is that as caught up in himself as he often seems to be, he is more than willing to give credit where credit is due when it comes to negotiating. When you are talking about negotiating with Donald Trump, then you are really talking about negotiating with his right-hand man: George Ross.

George has become famous in the last few years because he has appeared on Tump's TV show "The Apprentice" as Trump's advisor. However, George is really an experienced real estate lawyer who has worked with Trump since the 1970's.

He has been involved in hundreds of negotiations and is considered an expert in the field. In his book, Trump Style Negotiation, George lays out what Donald Trump believes that negotiation is NOT. Here they are:

1. **Once And For All, Negotiation Is NOT A Science:**
   George very clearly makes the point that negotiation is really just another form of communication between people. What everyone wants from a negotiation is a feeling of personal satisfaction when the final outcome is reached.

   This is critical because in negotiations we almost never end up with something that is tangible – that you can touch. Instead, it's the feeling that we walk away from the table with that determines how we judge the outcome.

2. **Just Forget About Winning – It's Not Everything:** If you see the world in terms of winners and losers then you are going to have trouble negotiating. The reason for this is that in negotiating, NOBODY wins or loses.

    Rather both sides give a little and gain a little in order to reach an agreement. This is why establishing trust with the other side of the table and building a friendly relationship are critical components of any good negotiating session.

3. **Negotiating Does Not Flow From Start To Finish:** Instead, it has a habit of starting, stopping, and then starting again. If you sit down at the negotiating table with the hope that you'll be able to knock out a final agreement in this one session, then more often than not you are going to be disappointed.

    One of the things that makes negotiating so hard to do well is the simple fact that since it stretches out over time, things change. Something that the other side said yesterday may no longer be true today. Hey, if negotiating was easy to do, then anyone could do it!

Understanding what negotiating is NOT is half the battle. Listen to the voice of experience and you will understand how to close more deals quicker.

# Chapter 9

# 10 Tips For Getting Satisfaction While Negotiating

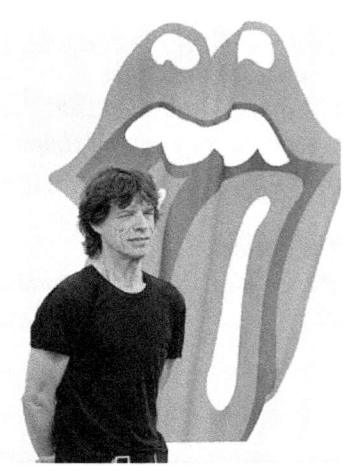

# Chapter 9: 10 Tips For Getting Satisfaction While Negotiating

Ok, so the title for this post is a bit screwy, but hopefully the point is clear: at the end of the day, negotiating is all about having both sides leave the negotiating table feeling satisfied. They may have had to give in on some things; however, in the end they both got what they really wanted. Now this all sounds fine and dandy, but just how does a negotiator go about making sure that everyone is going to become satisfied?

The first step is to realize that a negotiation is really just a specific type of relationship. Even as the world continues to change around us and new ways of doing business emerge such as outsourcing, strategic alliances, and partnerships one thing remains constant: negotiating is always needed.

However, how we actually go about negotiating is also undergoing a transformation. As both sides of the table now often have many partners in common, it makes sense to ensure that everyone has a good working relationship because undoubtedly we'll be doing business again in the future.

When we use the "R" word (relationship) this means that we are starting to talk about how satisfied each side of the table is with the deal that is being worked out. It goes without saying that depending on your actions you can either be building or diminishing the other side of the table's satisfaction. It is way too easy to diminish satisfaction so we'll focus on building satisfaction up.

There are two quick ways to do this. The first, interestingly enough, is to tell the other side "No" one more time. Whereas this does not at first seem to make sense, if you think about it you'll see that it really does.

In order for the other side of the table to feel as though they "got a deal", they also need to feel as though they worked for it. If they sat down, made a request, and you agreed to it, then they would leave the negotiating table feeling deeply dissatisfied.

The reason for this is because you didn't negotiate with them – they got something for nothing. Although you might think that this is the best possible outcome, it isn't . They won't be satisfied. However, if you say "No" then they'll need to work to reach a deal. Once a deal is reached, they will feel as though they "earned" a good deal.

The other way to ensure that the other side of the table leaves with a feeling of satisfaction, you need to remember the A.I.R. rule. A.I.R. stands for "**A**sk for something **I**n **R**eturn".

Never give up something for free. By asking for something in return, the other side of the table will feel that they "earned" what you gave to them.

In order to help you with the thinking about how best to ask for something in return, here is a list of things that you could ask for during most negotiations:

1. Better payment terms
2. A longer term contract
3. Who is responsible for delivery?
4. A freeze on prices
5. Most favored nation price guarantee
6. Have them buy additional products
7. Delivery options
8. Changes in staffing
9. Changes in specifications
10. Warranty

# Chapter 10

---

# 7 Ways To Be Successful In A Negotiation

## Chapter 10: 7 Ways To Be Successful In A Negotiation

If only there was some magic formula for being a successful negotiator. You know what I'm talking about, some process that if you followed it from start to finish you could always be assured that you would "win" a negotiation.

Well, the concept of winning a negotiation is a bit unclear. Rather we like to say that you want to come away from the negotiation feeling satisfied. Oh, and since a negotiation takes place between people who are infinitely complex and difficult to fully understand (yourself included), there is no way that any fixed formula is going to yield successful results every time. Rather, you need to be flexible and adapt your negotiating style to the current negotiation.

George Ross, who is Donald Trump's master negotiator, has come up with seven goals for how you can better your odds of succeeding in almost any negotiating situation. Considering how successful George has been, it sure seems like it might be worth the time to listen to what he has to share with us. That being said, here are the seven goals that you can keep in mind in order to be a successful negotiator:

1. **I Want To Find Ways To Get More Out Of This Negotiation**: The act of negotiating is a process of discovery for both sides. If you are able to distance yourself from narrowly focusing on just one point in the negotiation (price) and open your mind to all of the possibilities, then you will have a much better chance of being satisfied by the outcome of the negotiation.

2. **Learn, Learn, Lean (About The People On The Other Side Of The Table):** Why are they there? What do they want? Almost without fail what you think are the

answers to these questions turn out to be wrong. The only way that you are going to learn about the people who are sitting across from you is to start asking questions. Draw them out of themselves and who knows what valuable information will be revealed?

3. **Where Is The Bottom Line?:** At the end of the day, this is the critical question that all negotiators need to find an answer to. The other side has a minimum amount that they MUST get out of the negotiations and you have a maximum amount that you are willing to give up as a part of the negotiation. George calls the gap between these two amounts the "zone of uncertainty". Establishing the outline of this zone is what good negotiators do best.

4. **What Are The Constraints For This Deal?:** You have constraints put on you, the other side has the same. These constraints can be limits on the amount of time that is available to negotiate, how much decision making authority each side has, etc. Discovering what constraints the other side is dealing with can help move you towards a deal much quicker.

5. **Connect With The Other Side:** It is one of the great truths of life that we all like others who are most like us. What this means is that you need to find out as much about the other side of the table as quickly as you can. Once you have done this, you can start to interact with them in a way that they will most positively respond to.

6. **Understand The People Who Make Up Your Side Of The Table:** Nobody negotiates alone. You have a collection of people on your side while you are negotiating. They may not be in the room with you; however, they are the ones whose support allows you to be there and they all have a stake in the outcome of

the negotiations. They may not all agree with the posture that you are presenting to the other side of the table, but it's your job to hid any internal differences and present a single unified face.

7. **Discover What Is "Fair And Reasonable":** This poor phrase has been so overused by both sides of the negotiating table that it can often be ignored. However, don't do this. At the end of the day both sides of the table are searching for a deal that they believe is fair and reasonable. Unfortunately, we all define this slightly differently. Your job as a negotiator is to question and probe the other side of the table in order to find out how they define fair and reasonable. Then you will need to make sure that the deals that you propose to the other side meet these criteria so that they won't be rejected.

# Chapter 11

# 3 Steps To Building A Better Negotiation

## Chapter 11: 3 Steps To Building A Better Negotiation

If you really wanted to, you could go into any negotiation with your guns a-blazing and through dirty tricks, intimidation and other techniques probably get your way. However, you would have established a reputation as someone that nobody wants to do business with.

In the end, you would have lost much more than you would have gained. Instead, if you establish a reputation as a tough but fair negotiator whose word can be trusted, then everyone will want to do business with you.

Lots of people don't understand that during a negotiation you are really creating three different things: trust, rapport, and satisfaction. Instead of viewing a negotiation as a "winner takes all" type of competition, if you can view it as more of a construction project, then you'll be well on your way to being a successful negotiator.

Trust is a word that we all think that we know and understand; however, we are often too quick to dismiss it when it comes to establishing goals for a negotiation. The first rule of trust is don't even start to negotiate with someone that you don't trust – without this basic foundation, the discussions will end up going nowhere.

Sometimes when I'm working with people who are just starting out in negotiations, they make the mistake of associating trust with giving in to the other side's demands. No, no, no! During a negotiation you need to be pushing back, working to get what YOU want from the other side.

Just about any tactic (unless they are immoral or illegal) is permitted. However, when everything is said and done, you need to live up to your side of the agreement. Ultimately, this is what trust is all about.

Rapport sure sounds like something fancy, but in reality all it is a feeling that is deeper than trust. You can think about it as a form of being "tuned-in" to the other side of the table in such a way that you *understand* them.

When we are involved in a business negotiation, having rapport with the other side means that both sides respect each other, both sides actually like each other, and both sides are willing to do whatever it takes to make a deal happen.

The last bit of construction that needs to be done during a negotiation is to build satisfaction on both sides of the table. What this means is that it's actually very important for you to spend some time thinking about how the other side of the table is going to be feeling when they stand up after the negotiations are over.

If they are going to be feeling beaten down, betrayed, taken advantage of, or abused, then you have not done your job. Instead you've built a foe that will come back and cause you problems in the future.

This where the idea of being viewed as a "fair" negotiator comes in to play. When people deal with a fair negotiator they realize that they are going to have to give in on some items; however, they also expect to get their way on other items. In the end, they expect to walk away from the table with a sense of satisfaction that they were able to negotiate a good deal for themselves.

# Chapter 12

# 8 Ingredients For Baking A Delicious Negotiation

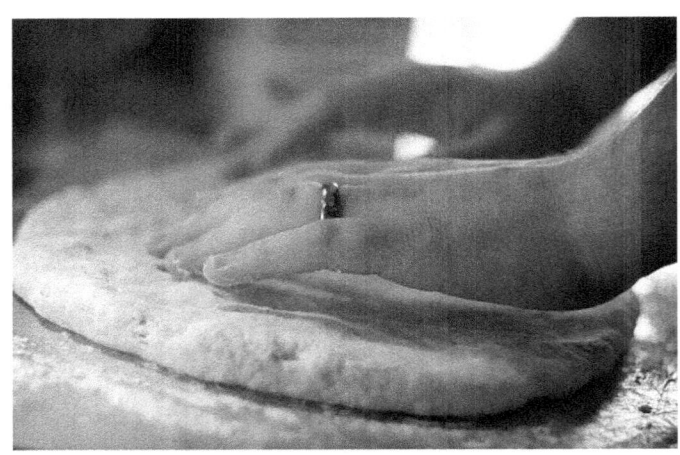

# Chapter 12: 8 Ingredients For Baking A Delicious Negotiation

And who wouldn't want to bake a delicious negotiation as long as they are going to go through the effort of conducting a negotiation anyway? In order for any negotiation to turn out successfully, YOU have a job to do. Specifically, you need to find ways to build trust, rapport, and satisfaction in the mind sitting across from you at the negotiating table. Got any thoughts on how best to do that?

Just in case you are still stuck on that old "I've got to WIN this negotiation" mentality, how about if we have a quick talk with our old friend George Ross who is Donald Trump's lead negotiator and ask him how best to do this type of negotiation baking. George suggests that we do the following 8 things in order to achieve our goals of building trust, rapport, and satisfaction:

1. **Locate Common Ground:** It doesn't matter just how far apart you feel that you are with the other side when you first sit down at the negotiating table, there is some common ground between you. Before you dive in and start talking about your differences, you should work with the other side in order find your common ground and then use that as a base to start your negotiations. Small talk, banter, looking at what someone displays in their office are all good ways to help you find this starting point.

2. **Visit The Rapport Store:** ... and make sure that you buy a whole bunch of rapport. This simply means that you need to make sure that the other side is comfortable talking with you (and that you are comfortable talking with them). This also means that you need to make sure

that the other side believes that you can fulfill any promises that you make to them.

3. **Just Be Nice:** Umm, this should be fairly obvious; however, lots of people try to put on their "negotiating face" in some sort of misguided attempt to scare the other side into giving in. Give it up. Be nice and you'll be amazed at what can happen.

4. **Match The Other Side:** What makes negotiations so "fun" is that we have to always be adjusting our negotiating style in order to match the other side and the current status of the negotiations. This is clearly a situation where "one size fits all" does NOT apply!

5. **Feel Their Pain:** Take the time to understand the other side of the table and think about what they are trying to accomplish. This is a critical part of making sure that you are going to be able to ensure that they will be satisfied as a result of the negotiations.

6. **Prove Yourself Worthy Of Trust:** Getting the other side to believe that they can trust you is difficult to do. Once done, you don't want to lose this trust during the negotiations. What this means is that you need to make sure that you keep any promises that you make during the negotiations.

7. **Bend, Don't Break:** Learning to be flexible is one of the key negotiation skills that the professionals have. Inflexibility spells doom for any negotiation because that can quickly become a deal breaker.

8. **Let Your Reputation Work For You:** If you are known as a deal maker, then the other side will come to the table with expectations of being able to successfully negotiate with you. If, on the other hand, you are

known as a deal breaker, then the other side will avoid having anything to do with you because they view negotiating with you as a waste of their time.

Hard work does not
guarantee success;
However, success does
not happen
without hard work.

— Dr. Jim Anderson

# Create An Effective Negotiating Team At Your Company!

Dr. Jim Anderson is available to provide training and coaching on the topics that are the most important to people who have to negotiate: how can my team effectively prepare for and execute a successful negotiation that will get us what we both want and need?

Dr. Anderson believes that in order to both learn and remember what he says, audiences need to laugh. Each one of his speeches is full of fun and humor so that what he says "sticks" with everyone.

### Dr. Anderson's Negotiating Training Includes:

1. How to plan for a negotiation: what information do you need and where can you find it?

2. What's the best way to explore how a deal can be created during a negotiation?

3. How can you bring a negotiation to a close without giving in to the other side?

Dr. Jim Anderson works with over 100 customers per year. To invite Dr. Anderson to work with you, contact him at:

**Phone: 813-418-6970** or
**Email: jim@BlueElephantConsulting.com**

Speaking.  Negotiating.  Managing.  Marketing.

# **Photo Credits:**

Cover - By: Tom Magliery
http://www.flickr.com/photos/mag3737/

Chapter 1 - By: king of monks
http://www.flickr.com/photos/kingofmonks/

Chapter 2 - By: prc1333
http://www.flickr.com/photos/pcw_1333/

Chapter 3 - By: reihayashi
http://www.flickr.com/photos/27629847@N03/

Chapter 4 - By: voguemarie2010
http://www.flickr.com/photos/49068459@N05/

Chapter 5 - By: arutha
http://www.flickr.com/photos/arutha/

Chapter 6 - By: Steev Hise
http://www.flickr.com/photos/steev/

Chapter 7 - By: Infrogmation of New Orleans
http://www.flickr.com/photos/infrogmation/

Chapter 8 - By: Gage Skidmore
http://www.flickr.com/photos/gageskidmore/

Chapter 9 - By: atlanticpublicity
http://www.flickr.com/photos/54805300@N07/

Chapter 10 - By: Dylan
http://www.flickr.com/photos/ekigyuu/

Chapter 11 - By: Peter Dutton
http://www.flickr.com/photos/joeshlabotnik/

Chapter 12 - By: Ginny
http://www.flickr.com/photos/ginnerobot/

www.ingramcontent.com/pod-product-compliance
Lightning Source LLC
Chambersburg PA
CBHW071819170526
45167CB00003B/1365